# LIVES IN CRISIS

# South Africa Since Apartheid

## SEAN SHEEHAN

HODDER
*Wayland*

an imprint of Hodder Children's Books

Published in Great Britain in 2002 by
Hodder Wayland, an imprint of Hodder Children's Books.

This book was prepared for Hodder Wayland by Ruth Nason.

Series concept: Alex Woolf
Series design: Carole Binding

Sean Sheehan asserts his right to be identified as author of this work,
in accordance with the Copyright, Designs and Patents Act 1988.

British Library Cataloguing in Publication Data
Sheehan, Sean, 1951-
    South Africa since apartheid. - (Lives in crisis)
    1. Apartheid - South Africa - History - Juvenile literature
    2. South Africa - Social conditions - 1994 - Juvenile literature
    3. South Africa - Politics and government - 1994 - Juvenile literature
I. Title
968'.065
ISBN 0 7502 4027 X

Printed in Hong Kong by Wing King Tong

Hodder Children's Books
A division of Hodder Headline Limited
338 Euston Road, London NW1 3BH

Cover (left) and page 1:
Nelson Mandela, president
of South Africa, announces
a cabinet reshuffle after the
National Party withdrew
from the government,
May 1996

## Acknowledgements

The Author and Publishers thank the following for their permission to
reproduce photographs: Camera Press: pages 27, 31, 50, 52, 57; Corbis
Images: cover background and pages 3 (Paul Velasco; Gallo Images),
4 (David Turnley), 5 (David Turnley), 6 (Peter Turnley), 9 (Peter Turnley),
10 (Hulton-Deutsch Collection), 11t (Underwood & Underwood),
11b (Peter Johnson), 13 (David Turnley), 14 (Hulton-Deutsch Collection),
15 (David Turnley), 19 (David Turnley), 20 (Peter Turnley), 22 (David
Turnley), 32 (Hulton-Deutsch Collection), 38 (David Turnley), 41
(Charles O'Rear), 46t (Caroline Penn), 49 (Charles O'Rear);
Popperfoto/AFP: pages 17, 18; Popperfoto/Reuters: cover portrait and
pages 1, 7, 8, 16, 23, 24, 25, 26, 28, 29, 30, 33, 34, 35, 36t, 36b, 39, 40,
42, 43, 44, 45, 46b, 47, 48t, 48c, 48b, 53, 54, 55, 56, 59.

# CONTENTS

South African football fans
wave their country's new flag.

# THE DAWN OF FREEDOM

Black South Africans queue to vote for the first time in their life, April 1994.

The election in South Africa that got underway on the morning of 26 April 1994 was no ordinary election. In previous general elections for new governments there, only white people – some 10 per cent of the population – had been allowed to vote. But now every adult in the country had the right to take part, whether white, black, Asian or of mixed descent. For the first time in South Africa's history, a government could be elected that would represent the interests of the majority of the population. Between 26 and 29 April, around twenty million black South Africans queued outside polling stations to make sure that this would be the case.

Television cameras, journalists and observers from all over the world were there, making it the most closely watched election of the twentieth century. Most of the world shared a sense of astonishment that the white leaders of a deeply racist country like South Africa were about to share power peacefully when the election results were announced. For decades, black people in South Africa had been shot for demanding equality.

## Queuing for the future

Maria Zulu, in her early 40s in 1994, remembers election day very clearly:

'I queued from nine in the morning until six at night – but if I had to, I would have stayed out until morning. I was very excited. I thought now things would happen. Not too much, but somewhat. A child doesn't just get up and walk. He starts sitting, then crawling and then walking and talking. You have to give him a chance. So I think we need to give the new government a chance.' (Quoted in *The Guardian*, 28 May 1999)

## Uncertainty and fear

As no election like this had ever taken place in South Africa before, there was uncertainty and fear as well as great hope for the future. There were no voter registration lists and it was unsure how many voters would turn up at each polling station. The first day of the election was set aside for the elderly, the infirm and pregnant mothers, because it seemed certain that long queues would develop on the other days. To prevent anyone trying to come back to vote a second time, election officials marked voters' fingers with a special ink that could only be detected under ultraviolet light.

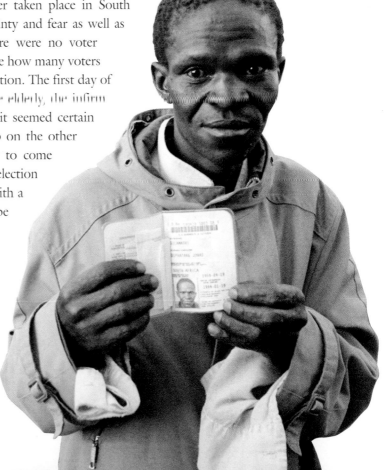

A voter shows his pass – a symbol of the old South Africa that black citizens were voting to change. Black South Africans could not travel freely around their own country and had to carry such passes with them.

## Just try

Patience Ndhlovu lived with her nine children in a one-room shack in a township area set aside for black South Africans. A week before the election, she told a journalist what she wished for the future:

'All I want is that Mandela should try for us. That is all. If he can try, then he will be doing more than the whites ever did.'
(Quoted in Keane, *The Bondage of Fear*)

Many people were alarmed about the possibility of violence and some feared that a bloodbath would spoil South Africa's first attempt to elect a democratic government. Previous governments had not only kept white and black people apart but also encouraged divisions between the non-white communities. The tensions created by these various divisions had already erupted into violence and there was great concern over what might happen once the election got underway.

Leader of the African National Congress, Nelson Mandela, campaigns for votes, April 1994. From 1962 to 1990 he was imprisoned for leading opposition to the white government.

On 24 April a massive car bomb, planted by white extremists in the city of Johannesburg, killed nine people. It was an attempt to frighten and demoralize voters. More bomb attacks took place on the 26th, including one that killed ten bystanders on a street.

A bomb attack on a taxi rank used by black people caused 10 deaths, in an eastern suburb of Johannesburg.

## Too much suffering

Anastasia Ncgobo, aged 68, explained her feelings on election day:

'Man, I could not sleep last night. I was tossing and turning, so I got up and stayed up, because this is a thing that only happens once and who was I to be able to sleep when we are going to vote?

I am here remembering all the people who suffered for this day, all of the children who was killed and Mr Mandela going to prison and the young boys who went into exile ... oh, it's too much, too much suffering has happened for this day. But in the end we know it was worth it. To be here and going to vote. I never thought I would see it in my lifetime.'
(Quoted in Keane, *The Bondage of Fear*)

During the counting of the votes, officials of the Independent Election Commission hold up ballot papers for party agents to verify.

Because of the fear of violence, over 100,000 police officers and thousands of army reservists were called on to help the security forces protect the polling stations. There were some 9,000 polling stations across the country. The whole election process was monitored by international election observers from the Independent Election Commission (IEC). Over 200,000 officials and volunteers administered the voting procedures, sealing up the ballot boxes after 29 April and arranging their secure transport to hundreds of counting centres. Here they were counted twice by hand before the results were agreed by the political parties and sent to the IEC to be entered into computers.

## A remarkable success

Despite the threat of violence and the challenge of administering an election where around 90 per cent of the population turned out to vote, three-quarters of them for the first time in their life, South Africa's first non-racial general election was a remarkable success. Voters started queuing in some areas as early as 1 a.m. on 26 April and an atmosphere of quiet calm was observed at most polling stations. Queues stretched for over a mile and some people spent 12 hours inching their way forward to the voting booths. Inevitably, various administrative problems arose, but on 30 April international observers confirmed that the elections had been free and fair.

## Voting for the ANC

Sipho 'Hotsticks' Mabhuza, a popular South African musician, explained the appeal of the ANC:

'People have been following it [the ANC] all their lives and before them their parents and their grandparents and so on back all the way to the beginning. It is a thing which is beyond politics and up at the top you have Mandela. You feel proud to belong to something like that.'
(Quoted in Keane, *The Bondage of Fear*)

## ANC victory

The African National Congress (ANC), the main party representing black voters, gained 63 per cent of the vote and a large majority of seats in the new parliament. Another party supported by black voters, the Inkatha Freedom Party (IFP), won 10 per cent of the vote. The National Party, representing white voters, gained 20 per cent of the vote. Many Asians and people of mixed descent also voted for the National Party, because they did not want an overwhelming victory for the ANC. Nelson Mandela, the new president of his country, called the ANC victory the 'dawn of our freedom' and a 'small miracle' – but in political terms it was a very big miracle.

Singing to celebrate Mandela's inauguration as president, this choir are dressed in robes designed after the new South African flag.

# THE RISE AND FALL OF APARTHEID

The earlier history of South Africa helps to explain why the April 1994 election was such a momentous event, surprising many South Africans as much as it surprised the rest of the world.

## The arrival of European colonists

The first colonists to settle in southern Africa were a group of Dutch people, who arrived in the middle of the seventeenth century. They pushed into the interior, establishing farms and fighting with the native population. These Dutch farmers became known as Boers. In the meantime, the British arrived and conquered the coastal tip of southern Africa. The Boers were upset and, in a journey called 'the Great Trek', several thousand of them headed north in search of new lands. They formed two independent states: the Transvaal and the Orange Free State. When diamond and gold deposits were discovered in the interior in the nineteenth century, this brought the British and the Boers into open conflict. Their three-year war ended in 1902 with the defeat of the Boers.

Boer soldiers in a trench outside Mafeking. The Boers besieged the British in Mafeking, from October 1899 to May 1900.

The arrival of the Dutch and British severely disrupted the way of life of the native black population of southern Africa. The colonists defeated the natives in battle, as they had superior weapons, and, in time, land shortages forced young black men to find employment in the expanding mining industry.

## The founding of South Africa

By the end of the nineteenth century, European powers had carved up the whole of southern Africa between them and in 1910 the British founded the modern state of South Africa. The Boers, also known as Afrikaners, formed their own political party in 1914 and called it the National Party. Although under British rule, the Afrikaners made up the majority of whites in South Africa, and they became the dominant force, since voting rights were not given to black people even though they made up the overwhelming majority of the population.

## Creating apartheid

From the earliest days of South Africa, its governments introduced and enforced laws to prevent non-whites from gaining political or economic equality with white people. Apartheid, an Afrikaner word meaning 'separateness', became the South African term for the government's system of treating whites and non-whites as different groups of people. The foundations for such a system were laid under British rule, but when the Afrikaner National Party gained power in 1948 they extended the policies in a number of ways. All South Africans were classified into one of four racial groups: whites, blacks,

Diamond mine workers, Kimberley, in the 1940s.

Harvesting grapes for wine. The law made it impossible for blacks to own farming land where they could be self-sufficient. They became dependent on white farmers for their living.

Asians (who were mostly Indians), and those of mixed descent who were officially labelled 'coloureds'. Blacks – over three-quarters of the population – were divided again into ten tribal groups and each group was allocated its own 'homeland'. These 'homelands' were scattered, relatively poor areas of land and they were anything but 'home' to many people who were then forced to move there. For the black population in urban areas, the white government created large, densely packed communities known as townships. The largest of these, just outside Johannesburg, was named South-Western Township, which became shortened to Soweto.

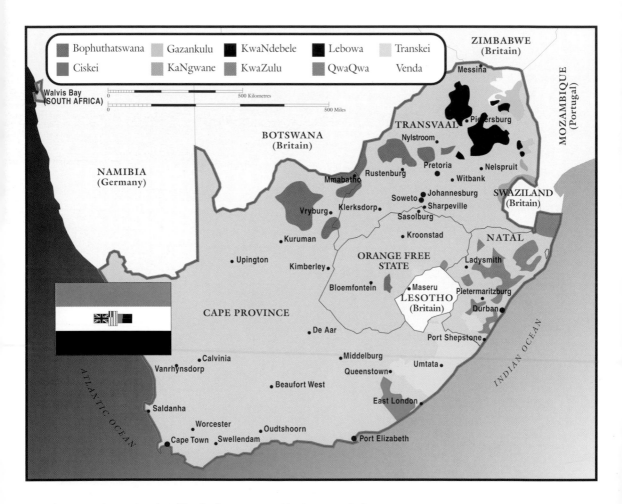

This map shows South Africa before 1994, with the ten tribal areas created for black people. Neighbouring countries have the name of the colonial power that once governed them in brackets. For a long time, the landlocked states of Lesotho and Swaziland were expected to become part of South Africa, but this never happened.

Under a variety of apartheid laws – more than 15,000 regulations and 200 separate laws by 1994 – the white minority in South Africa created a privileged life for themselves, while denying non-whites many of the most basic human rights. Mixed-race marriages were not allowed, and buses, parks, sporting events and other aspects of everyday life were segregated along racial lines.

A family at home in KwaZulu, 1994.

Black people had to live in their 'homelands' and carry passes whenever they needed to travel outside of them. The far-flung location of many homelands meant that many blacks frequently had to make long journeys to find employment in white areas. Often, black people had little choice but to live in special accommodation blocks near to their place of work but away from their families. Most households in the 'homelands' were living in poverty, and disease and malnutrition were common.

## Apartheid

Sandra Liang, with white parents and two white brothers, was born dark skinned and became more black as she grew up. By an accident of her genes, inter-breeding in the distant past between blacks and whites had produced this unusual case.

'In 1966, when I was 10, the police came to take me away from my school. Mr Van Tonder, the principal, said I was not white and could not stay ... I felt a lot of pain and thought it would be best if I left and stayed with people I felt happier with.'

Rejected by her community and her local church, Sandra married a black and was disowned by her parents. She was finally reunited with her mother thirty years later. (Quoted in *The Guardian*, January 2000)

## A South African joke

'God called St Peter to witness his finest creation.
"Mountains that pierce the sky, great forests that shelter all manner of
wondrous creatures, endless plains and deserts and grasslands ... All these
things shall this land have ... And beneath the mountains and rivers a
treasure trove of gold and diamonds, platinum and uranium."
Peter said this was wonderful, but wouldn't South Africans be the envy of
every other nation on earth?
"No, they won't," God said. "Wait till you see the government I'm going
to give them." '
(Quoted in Bell, *Somewhere Over the Rainbow*)

### Opposing apartheid

The reality of apartheid made itself known to the outside world
in 1960, when news broke that South African police had
opened fire on a group of people in Sharpeville protesting at
the pass laws. Sixty-nine people were killed but, when
criticized by other countries, the South African government
only hardened its attitude. In 1961, South Africa left the

More than 50 people lie
dead after police opened
fire on a demonstration in
Sharpeville, 1960.

Commonwealth and became an independent republic, while within the country the African National Congress (ANC), an organization campaigning for equal rights, was declared illegal. The ANC was not the only body opposing apartheid inside South Africa but it was the most organized and it now decided that violence should be used to force change on the government. In 1962, a number of ANC leaders were imprisoned, including a young man called Nelson Mandela.

Opposition to apartheid broke out again in 1976, in Soweto. The authorities opened fire on schoolchildren who were marching against attempts to force them to study in Afrikaans, the language of the Boers. Sixteen were killed. Ten years later, South Africa was in a state of widespread insurrection and protests were organized to try to make the townships ungovernable. Black trade unions launched a series of strikes, rent strikes also took place, and the ANC increased its armed struggle. The government tried

During the 1980s, a whole generation of young people, like this man carrying a fire bomb, felt they had little option but to take part in violent protest against apartheid.

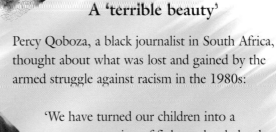

## A 'terrible beauty'

Percy Qoboza, a black journalist in South Africa, thought about what was lost and gained by the armed struggle against racism in the 1980s:

'We have turned our children into a generation of fighters, battle-hardened soldiers who will never know the carefree joy of childhood. What we are witnessing is the growth of a generation which has the courage to reject the cowardice of its parents ... There is a dark, terrible beauty in that courage. It is also a source of great pride.'
(Quoted in Murray, *The Revolution Deferred*)

## Vigils and funerals

Miriam, a secondary-school student, described life in the mid-1980s:

'The police no longer issue warnings before shooting. We are burying people every weekend. During periods of unrest in the past, we'd been allowed to bury our dead with relative dignity. Now the police issue new guidelines for funerals ... If we disregard the restrictions and turn out in waves, the police are there in their armoured trucks. At the end of the funeral they often spray us with tear gas to disperse us, or open fire, and this leads to more night vigils and funerals.'
(Quoted in Mathabane, *Miriam's Song*)

In November 1985 as many as 100,000 people took part in an anti-apartheid demonstration in London.

to control the situation by armed force, and terribly brutal acts led to a spiral of increasing violence. Black leaders were tortured and killed in prison, protesters were shot in the streets, and the system of apartheid came under severe pressure. International protests also began to make themselves felt, and banks in North America and Western Europe threatened to withhold loans to South Africa.

# A problem with killing

Looking back, Harold Snyman, a white policeman, tried to explain why he had killed three black ANC supporters.

'Personally, I had problems with the killing of people. But I came to the conclusion that the only way forward was for these three people to be eliminated ... I had problems with my conscience, and, as a Christian, I could not reconcile myself to this sort of action. At that stage we executed the policy of the government.'
(Quoted in *The Guardian*, 26 November 1997)

## Inkatha and the ANC

To try to weaken the insurrection, the South African government made deals with the black leaders of some of the 'homelands'. Some black leaders were willing to work against the ANC and would reduce opposition to the government, in return for economic advantages for their territory and a guarantee that they would keep their local power. This government policy was most effective in KwaZulu, where the Inkatha party set out to defeat the ANC by violent means.

Supporters of the Inkatha Freedom Party march through Thokoza township, September 1991.

## The end of apartheid

By the end of the 1980s it was obvious that South Africa had to change. In 1989 a new leader of the National Party, F. W. de Klerk, became president of the country and he quickly announced sweeping changes that would remove most of the apartheid laws. In 1990 de Klerk announced that the ANC would no longer be an illegal organization and that its leaders, including Mandela, would be released from prison.

How had such an astonishing turnabout taken place? One reason was the success of the insurrection by angry black people, a rebellion that could only be kept in check by brutal force. Another reason was the gradual ending of the long-drawn-out 'Cold War' between the USA and the USSR. While the Cold War lasted, the USA and other Western states had always been willing to support South Africa, because it strongly defended capitalism and allied itself with the West. But in the late 1980s, as the Cold War drew to a close, Western powers and multinational banks were less prepared to support the unpopular racist state. They were more willing to listen to the international protests calling for the isolation of South Africa. Economic and political pressure from the West helped make it obvious to de Klerk's government that the apartheid system would have to be dismantled if the white minority was to hold on to some of its power and privileges.

President F. W. de Klerk listens as Nelson Mandela delivers a speech about their talks, May 1990.

There was also a change in the attitude of the ANC. For a long time it had been feared that, if the ANC were given power, it would promote socialist policies that would remove the privileges enjoyed by white people. The negotiations that took place after 1990 between de Klerk's government and the ANC convinced the white leaders that the ANC would not reject capitalism and that it would be possible to make a deal.

Nelson Mandela was a key factor in making such a deal possible because, despite his 27 years in prison, he was remarkably free of bitterness. He won the trust of many whites with his ability to put to one side the long history of humiliation and violence against black people. More importantly, he convinced white leaders that the ANC would not introduce socialist reforms such as redistributing wealth from the wealthy to the needy.

The government under de Klerk had to convince its white supporters that sharing power with the ANC would not mean the

Trainee members of the white extremist *Afrikaner Werstandsbeweging* (African Resistance Movement) at a rally in 1994.

sudden collapse of their way of life. They were largely successful but not completely so, and small groups of white extremists formed parties with the intention of resisting any compromise with the ANC. In an unlikely alliance, neo-Nazi white supremacists found themselves on the same side as the black Inkatha party who also opposed a deal between the government and the ANC. Inkatha supporters were worried that they would lose power and influence if the ANC formed the next government of South Africa. White racists within the South African police and army worked with Inkatha groups, training men to attack and kill members of the ANC.

Negotiations lasted from 1990 until 1994, when eventually an agreement was reached that led to South Africa's first non-racial general election. With the ANC the clear winner, Mandela became the new president of the country. Before 1994, the government had used Impala and Mirage jets to bomb ANC fighters labelled 'terrorists'. During the 1994 public ceremony to transfer power to the ANC, these same jets flew overhead and tipped their wings to acknowledge their new commander – former 'terrorist' prisoner, now President Nelson Mandela.

South Africa was to make a fresh start, but past history would weigh heavily on the future.

## A change of heart?

Colin Nkabinde, aged 21, knew that South Africa had become a different country after the election of 1994 but wondered if white people had really changed:

'I know things have changed because I can eat with white people if I want. But for many of them, I don't think things have changed in their hearts. They still don't like black people.'
(Quoted in *The Guardian*, 28 May 1999)

# INHERITING THE PAST

## National Unity?

The biggest problem facing the new, multiracial government of South Africa in 1994 was the legacy of the past. In some respects, such as its railways and roads and wealth of natural resources, South Africa could match high-income countries and present itself as a modern, prosperous nation. But in most key areas of life – education, housing, health, land ownership and employment – there were enormous difficulties, all created by apartheid. Removing apartheid laws was easy; in fact, de Klerk's government before 1994 had already removed most of the racist legislation. Removing the inequalities that had been created by these laws was a much greater challenge.

Nelson Mandela, a Xhosa, shakes hands with the Zulu king Goodwill Zwelithini. F. W. de Klerk is on the left, and Chief Mangosuthu Buthelezi of the Inkatha party is on the right. Despite the handshakes, the legacy of the past had created bitterness between the ethnic groups of South Africa.

The deal negotiated before the 1994 election included an agreement that a Government of National Unity would first be created. This government would be made up of all the parties gaining over 20 seats in the election, in proportion to their share of the vote. So, although the ANC won the 1994 election with 63 per cent of the vote, the new government also included members of the National Party (NP) – the white minority party that had once ruled the country – and members of the Inkatha party from KwaZulu.

Although the majority of blacks in South Africa are Xhosa people, there are also Zulu people. The Zulus are proud of their history because in the nineteenth century their strong kingdom had resisted the British and the Boers. They had a strong sense of identity. The Inkatha party had become powerful by claiming to represent the interests of the Zulus, but the ANC had little respect for the Inkatha leaders because of the way they had been willing to work with white extremists (see page 19). After the 1994 election, the Inkatha leader, Mangosuthu Buthelezi, was not trusted because of his attempts to increase his own power, and violent encounters between ANC and Inkatha supporters caused more bloodshed. All this was happening while Buthelezi was a leading member of the new Government of National Unity!

The fact that the NP had been able to negotiate a pre-election deal that gave them a say in the new government of the

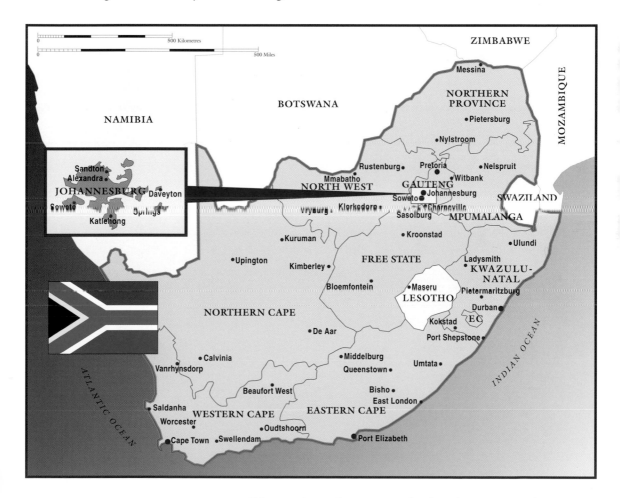

This map shows the 'new' South Africa that emerged after the election of 1994. Lesotho and Swaziland remain independent states but their economies are very dependent on South Africa.

By 1995 some things had changed. A fruit farmer takes tea with two of his labourers, but a black woman is still employed as housemaid.

country reflected the economic power still wielded by the white minority. After all, South Africa had been run by the NP for nearly 50 years in order to keep economic power in the hands of white people. While the 1994 election gave black people political power, it did nothing to change the white ownership of farming land, gold mines and powerful companies. The multiracial election made some whites feel liberated, like the shopkeeper who exclaimed after the election, 'Isn't this bloody marvellous? For the first time in my life I don't feel ashamed of being white.' However, the election

## Radio for a rainbow

Radio South Africa, an English-language station which used to broadcast to whites, changed its name to SAfm and set out to attract a black audience as well. It began to play black music and use black DJs who could relate to a wider audience. One white listener likened the change to Nazi domination:

'What they have done is impose their will on us. You vill listen to Black music and mangled Black English, ve haf vays and means!'

The radio station manager defended SAfm: 'We are catching a lot of flak from arrogant white English speakers. These people cannot come to terms with the exciting new rainbow society we are trying to create.'
(Quoted in Arnold, *The New South Africa*)

## Different vibes

Pieter 'Hempies' du Toit is a rural Afrikaner who can trace his family back six generations to French immigrants. After the 1994 election, he noticed a change in the attitude of the black people he employed on his farm:

'Things have changed a bit. My people have joined the union, and the vibes are different. In the past you felt they put their trust in you as their employer, now they look elsewhere and the relationship is not the same.'
(Quoted in Bell, *Somewhere Over the Rainbow*)

result made no change to the deeply ingrained racism of the many whites who did not share such feelings. Many whites accepted the changes of 1994 because they felt there was little alternative, rather than because of any heartfelt commitment to a more just society. An example of this was revealed early in 1995 when a group of whites used guns, whips and dogs to try to prevent children from a township near Cape Town from entering what had previously been an all-white school. A year later, 200 white parents tried to bar black six-year-olds from a primary school. In 1996, when the country's first black judge was appointed, 100 judges, including all ten in the Appeal Court, opposed the appointment.

The ANC knew well that racist attitudes had not evaporated just because non-racial elections had taken place. For them, the task of planning for the future was made more difficult both by the tensions between itself, the NP and Inkatha, and by the daunting legacy of racism.

Cape Town, February 1995: a group of right-wingers threaten black pupils attending a school that was once for whites only. They are holding South Africa's pre-1994 flag.

June 1994, in a settlement
east of Johannesburg.

## 'Now where is my house?'

Even before the election of 1994, a woman named Khayelitsha, from a squatter settlement outside Cape Town, wrote to her local newspaper and asked 'Now where is my house?' Black people looked to the ANC to improve the material conditions of life. For decades they had endured humiliation, hardship and deprivation, and they had voted overwhelmingly to bring the ANC to power because they wanted change. Ordinary black people had a very poor standard of living and a typical family in 1994 lived on a meagre diet of maize and porridge, supplemented by vegetables that could be grown in a garden. Their budget allowed them to buy meat about once a month. Many families struggled to meet the cost of sending their children to school.

## A typical day

'I get up at four in the morning and go down to the river to fetch the water. This can take up to two hours as the river is usually dry and I have to dig to get clean water and it takes long to fill my container [20 litres].

I return to clean the baby and heat the water for the gogo [grandmother] to wash with. I then prepare some food for the family – this is usually porridge and tea. I then go to the fields to water my crops and dig up any weeds ... When I return I start cooking the evening meal. We cook with an open fire and I collect the wood from the forest at the weekends. After cooking and feeding the baby, I wash and clean and then go to sleep about six; but this can be later in the summer when we are busier.'
(Quoted in May, ed., *Poverty and Inequality in South Africa*)

## Unemployment

No accurate figures are available, but between 20 and 40 per cent of employable people were without a job in 1994 and poorer people had the least chance of being in work. In Alexandra township, at the time of the election, the unemployment rate was 65 per cent. At the beginning of 1995, the civil service advertised over 10,000 jobs for clerks, cleaners and managers and a staggering 1.5 million applications were received for these posts.

Since the release of Mandela in 1990, thousands of ANC activists and guerrilla fighters had returned to South Africa from exile in neighbouring countries. They hoped to find employment, but their experience and skills often did not match those needed in peacetime jobs.

### Coming home

A widow of over 70, Gelle Tshabalala returned to South Africa after 35 years in exile. She found herself foraging for food in dustbins in central Johannesburg:

'When we were in exile, the ANC looked after us. They promised when we came back to South Africa in 1991 they would educate our children and provide housing and money. Since we returned home, the ANC has not given us anything. What can I do? I am too old for work and often I am sick.'
(Quoted in *Gemini News Service*, 15 May 1998)

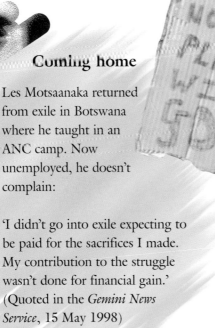

### Coming home

Les Motsaanaka returned from exile in Botswana where he taught in an ANC camp. Now unemployed, he doesn't complain:

'I didn't go into exile expecting to be paid for the sacrifices I made. My contribution to the struggle wasn't done for financial gain.'
(Quoted in the *Gemini News Service*, 15 May 1998)

On a street corner in Johannesburg.

### Schools

The education system, suffering from decades of apartheid, was in dire need of attention. Under successive white governments, ten times more money was spent on the education of white children than on black. Over 80 per cent of schools lacked a library, over half lacked electricity and a telephone, one quarter managed without a water supply and more than one in ten had no toilets.

## Race and health

The figures below show how standards of health varied according to race.

|  | White | Coloured | Asian | Black |
|---|---|---|---|---|
| Percentage of deaths at 5 years and younger | 12 | 19 | 13 | 20 |
| Male life expectancy at birth, 1990 | 69 | 59 | 64 | 60 |
| Female life expectancy at birth, 1990 | 76 | 65 | 70 | 67 |

(Quoted in May, ed., *Poverty and Inequality in South Africa*)

Waiting for treatment at a hospital in Northern Province, 1999.

## Health care

The system of health care had improved in the early 1990s but there were still dreadful inequalities based on race. The Northern Province was one of the better-provided regions but in 1996 it had only 290 doctors employed in public hospitals for a population of some 6 million. In fact, the situation was even more alarming than this, since only 20 of these doctors were South African citizens.

There was also the particular problem of an AIDS epidemic, which was increasing at a frightening pace. One year after the election, 2 per cent of the country – 850,000 individuals – were estimated to be HIV-positive and this rate was projected to almost double every year. In spite of this, amongst the general public, there was a great deal of ignorance and misunderstanding about AIDS.

In 1999 goods on sale at this shop in Johannesburg included the African potato, wrongly believed to be a cure for HIV and AIDS.

## Dying from AIDS

Mrs Nkabule, 32, lives in Alexandra township and from her home she has a view of Sandton, an expensive shopping district where only wealthy whites are seen. She has three young children and is HIV-positive, but cannot afford the drugs available in Sandton City.

'If you go to the clinic here they tell you they can give you some pills to make you feel better, but they tell us that we must brace ourselves to die because there is nothing they can do ... What will happen to my children when I am dead?'
(Quoted in *The Guardian*, 30 November 2000)

## Other issues to tackle

A major issue to be tackled was that of restoring land to people who had been forcibly removed during the years of apartheid. People were given four years from the month of the election to lodge their claims and some 16,000 claims on land were submitted in the first three years.

As well as this, there was the forbidding prospect of dealing with the poor housing and social problems in the large townships, like the region around Johannesburg where almost one quarter of the country's population lived.

So near but so far: living in a shack on the edge of Cape Town, with a view of the modern, well-off city.

## The economy

To attend to all these urgent problems the government needed large amounts of money. Houses had to be built, water and electricity brought to people's homes, jobs created, a health service and an education service made available to everyone, and a host of other matters dealt with. In the past, the ANC had had plans to take over some of South Africa's highly profitable businesses and redistribute their wealth to remedy the social problems. The justification for such measures was that 40 per cent of households, amounting to nearly 20 million people, were struggling to live on a monthly income of around £35. However, during the negotiations before the election, the white government had secured agreement from the ANC that such radical policies would not be pursued. So, instead, the country went out of its way to stress to the Western world that it was 'business as usual'. While this helped to make the transition of power remarkably peaceful, it presented the ANC with the problem of maintaining an economic system which was responsible for many of the country's difficulties.

To make matters worse, in the last years of apartheid, the South African economy had taken a nose-dive. International protests had succeeded in isolating the country and pressurizing banks and multinational companies not to invest in South Africa. More capital was leaving the country than coming into it, international debts had accumulated, and the economy was growing at a slow rate. The apartheid state had also built up an over-large bureaucracy, creating comfortable jobs for white people – and the pre-1994 negotiations included an ANC agreement to guarantee jobs for all apartheid officials in the civil service.

Most of South Africa's problems stemmed from the inequality that had been created and sustained under apartheid. Just 5 per cent of the population owned 88 per cent of the wealth; few other countries in the world, if any, had such a lopsided distribution of wealth. Around 50,000 white farmers owned 85 per cent of agricultural land. Class and race came together, with the poor being mostly black and the rich mostly white. Better-off households spent over six times more money on food each year than poor families.

Combing a rubbish tip for scraps of food – a daily routine for this woman from a squatter settlement outside Johannesburg.

### Average incomes, South Africa, 1995
R = Rands

Whites: R103,000 (£9,500)
Asians: R71,000 (£6,500)
Coloureds: R32,000 (£3,000)
Blacks: R23,000 (£2,100)

A wall in Johannesburg has been declared a memorial, in honour of all those killed in recent car hijackings and other violent crimes. Fifteen artists volunteered their time to paint portraits of some of the thousands of people murdered, May 1997.

## Inheriting violence

The four days of the 1994 election were remarkably peaceful, but the new South Africa that emerged from it had inherited years of violence. The white government of de Klerk had routinely employed violence and assassinations to try to crush the resistance movement against apartheid, and this had led to more violence as people fought back. Also, Inkatha party supporters had been trained by government forces to attack the ANC, and so political violence was commonplace, and continued even after 1994. Between 1984 and 1997 an average of 2,000 political killings took place in South Africa every year.

The lawlessness carried on. After April 1994, an average of one murder, two rapes and more than twelve house burglaries happened in South Africa every half an hour. Social divisions and high unemployment resulted in a soaring crime rate in the city of Johannesburg, where the wealthy lived in homes protected by high walls and 'instant armed response' security companies while the poor were in slum, shanty towns like Alexandra. Johannesburg earned a reputation as one of the world's most dangerous cities, and South Africa was regarded as the most dangerous place in the world outside a war zone. In Soweto, guns were available for rent by the hour. The lack of effective policing was another consequence of apartheid, with over 80 per cent of the police concentrated in white areas.

The lawlessness was also an after-effect of the civil disobedience that blacks had mounted to oppose apartheid. During the late 1980s, when the ANC set out to make the townships ungovernable, 'liberation before education' had become a battle cry as school strikes disrupted the school system. Young people became politicized, angry, and sometimes armed. It was difficult for this generation of young people to adapt to the South Africa that was trying, peacefully, to re-invent itself after 1994.

After his factory was robbed 40 times in four years, this man bought two pythons to guard the premises.

## The legacy of violence

Nomavende Mathiane, a black journalist living in Soweto, understands why many young blacks turned to violence.

'They were faced with a tough world where the game was always played according to the white man's rules. If the white man had to destroy to survive, to stave off whatever bleak future the black youth seemed to be orchestrating for him, he used violence to try and stop it. And the children learned to retaliate with violence.' (Quoted in Keane, *The Bondage of Fear*)

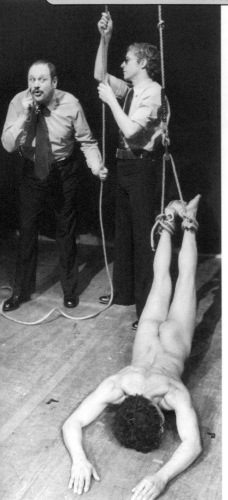

# TRUTH AND RECONCILIATION?

The Government of National Unity that ruled after April 1994 had to draw up a new constitution for South Africa's future. There was also a need to deal with the country's painful past, the years of apartheid when non-whites had been denied basic human rights and been persecuted for opposing the all-white government.

## Making space for the future

Victims of persecution, or their families in cases where the victims had been murdered, called for justice. For example, the family of Steve Biko, a black leader in the late 1970s who was beaten to death while manacled in a police cell, wanted people like his murderers to be tried and punished. While some demanded retribution, others thought it would be better to

A scene from a play, *Mr Biko*,
performed at the Round House
Theatre in London in March 1979:
two security police beat Steve Biko.

## Steve Biko's death

The policemen who applied for amnesty for the killing of Steve Biko had their application rejected. A main reason for this was the policemen's unwillingness to provide an honest account of what happened. This is clear from evidence like the following, meant to show the TRC that Biko's death was an accident:

'During the course of the scuffle there were blows being exchanged, although nobody is really certain whether any of these blows landed and ... in the process of the scuffle, Mr Biko lost his balance ... It was noted that Mr Biko appeared to be, one could use the word stunned, confused.'
(*Hearing of the Truth and Reconciliation Committee*, 10 September 1997, Port Elizabeth)

draw a veil over the past. They argued that recalling past injustices could harm South Africa's ability to make a fresh start; it would be better to encourage amnesia in the interests of stability. Not surprisingly, members of the former white government and its security forces did not relish the idea of being held to account for past atrocities. An amnesty was part of the deal negotiated before the 1994 election.

Accordingly, the new constitution called for the establishment of a Truth and Reconciliation Commission. This would make public the injustices committed during the struggle against apartheid, and amnesty would be granted to those who made a full confession of past political crimes.

The seventeen members of the Truth and Reconciliation Commission (TRC) began their first hearing in April 1996. For the following two years, in locations around the country, witnesses were called to give evidence about past atrocities. Over 20,000 statements were taken from victims – 2,000 of them in public hearings, and nearly 8,000 people applied for amnesty. The TRC was not a court of law and did not seek to establish guilt or innocence, but it could reject an amnesty application. It hoped that the promise of amnesty would encourage those who carried out terrible deeds to make a full confession. The idea was that by clearing the air in this way, space would be created for racial reconciliation in the future.

The chairman and deputy chairman of the Truth and Reconciliation Commission: Archbishop Desmond Tutu (right) and Alex Boraine.

## Uncomfortable truths

There is no doubt that the TRC brought uncomfortable and painful truths into the open. Television and newspapers highlighted stories from TRC witnesses, both victims and perpetrators, which clearly established how black people had been persecuted, to the extent of torture and murder, by the security forces of the apartheid regime. It was revealed that South African scientists were researching ways of developing bacteria that would harm only blacks, as well as ways of controlling black fertility so as to limit the black population.

Many white South Africans were shocked to discover what had been committed in their name. They felt uncomfortable when they heard people like Wouter Mentz, a security policeman,

## Photographs

One policeman admitted taking part in the killing of a black woman and identified her grave. The written record of the TRC hearing describes his reaction when shown a photograph of the ground where she was buried:

' "She was brave this one, hell she was brave," says the grave indicator, the perpetrator, and whistles softly through his teeth. "She simply would not talk."

Another photograph is shown of the woman's bones. Around the pelvis is a blue plastic bag.

"Oh yes," the grave indicator remembers. "We kept her naked and after ten days she made herself these panties." He sniggers: "God ... she was brave." ' (Quoted in Krog, *Country of My Skull*)

The start of a hearing, August 1997. Janusz Walus (left) and Clive Derby-Lewis (right) were seeking a pardon for the assassination of a communist party leader, Chris Hani. Their lawyers stand between them.

describing in detail how black people were murdered and claiming that 'people slept safe while we were fighting terrorists'. Many whites denied knowing what was happening. They included the former President F. W. de Klerk, who stated to the Commission that he had never authorised acts of torture or murder. This annoyed other whites, especially those accused of attacking the ANC, who claimed that the government knew very well what the security forces were doing.

Journalists Thami Mazwai (left) and John Qwelane are sworn in before a special hearing on the media. They accused South African newspapers of manipulating the news to support the apartheid government.

The Truth and Reconciliation Commission also confronted terrible misdeeds committed by black people during the struggle against apartheid. For example, anyone suspected of giving information against blacks to the security forces ran the risk of 'necklacing': a car tyre filled with petrol was placed around the victim's neck and set alight.

## Necklacing

Nozibele Madubedube's sister died as a result of necklacing and Nozibele also had a tyre put around her neck, but was saved by a neighbour who intervened and insisted she was not an informer against the ANC. Nozibele was traumatized:

'I was alive, but also not. If any light flickers anywhere, I instinctively think it's fire. My whole family is … just partly alive … When we're driving in the car, I look at my husband and children and I feel … I see them … and I do not see them at all … when I touch them it feels as if there is a thick skin over my hands … especially my oldest child always seems to be afraid of me … I sat in front of the Truth Commission, I saw two of those who grabbed me and my sister in the hall … and they are still … nothing … only … now I am also nothing. My life keeps slipping through my fingers.'
(Quoted in Krog, *Country of My Skull*)

One story of an ANC-related murder created dramatic headlines because it concerned Nelson Mandela's former wife, Winnie Mandela. The TRC heard how her personal bodyguards, the so-called Mandela Football Club, acted like gangsters while claiming to fight apartheid. They had murdered young men on her orders. It was difficult for black society to come to terms with witnesses' reports to the TRC that teenagers like Stompie Seipei, whose mutilated body was found on waste ground after he had been kidnapped by the Mandela Football Club, had been tortured and killed on the orders of Winnie Mandela.

## Reconciliation?

The TRC hoped that, after bringing uncomfortable truths about the past into the open, people would be able to move forward with their lives. 'We cannot move forward until we know everything that has happened. And then learn to forgive, if not forget,' wrote a South African newspaper at the time. Something like this seemed to be happening when witnesses came forward with details of tortures, bombings,

Winnie Mandela takes the oath at a TRC hearing in December 1997. It was said that she had given orders for the murder of Stompie Seipei (top).

kidnappings, murders and secret burials. Sometimes, members of the security forces who committed these deeds broke down and asked for forgiveness. 'I have decided to stop apologising for apartheid and to tell the truth,' announced William Harrington, a policeman who hunted down ANC supporters. Some victims, and relatives of murdered victims, accepted pleas for forgiveness and felt able to leave the past in the past. Some found this impossible, like a mother whose son had been

## Living in a nightmare

Yazir Henry betrayed his comrade to the security police who threatened to kill his mother and four-year-old nephew. He explains to the TRC:

'I was 19. I don't think anyone in the world should have been given such a choice. The brutality and the tenacity with which they questioned me, and my knowledge of what they had done to others ... made their threat to kill my family very real ... I just want to be judged for who I am, that's all. I just want to be given a chance to start life again – I've been living in a nightmare.'
(Quoted in Villa-Vicencio and Verwoerd, *Looking Back Reaching Forward*)

burnt alive by the security forces: 'In my life,' she said 'not a single thing has changed since my son was burnt by barbarians ... nothing. Therefore I cannot forgive.'

The chairperson of the TRC, Archbishop Desmond Tutu, played a crucial role in emphasizing the need for forgiveness. Sometimes, as when he brought the mother of Stompie face to face with Winnie Mandela, the act of public reconciliation was not convincing. Mrs Mandela never admitted her role in the murder of people like Stompie, even though the evidence looked conclusive.

## Telling the truth

James Bisholo, an unemployed black South African, values what the TRC stands for.

'I know about the TRC, they tell the truth there. Old men like President Mandela and Archbishop Tutu tell the truth and shame the devil. That's all I know.'
(Quoted in Villa-Vicencio and Verwoerd, *Looking Back Reaching Forward*)

P. W. Botha was president of South Africa from 1984 to 1989.

The whole endeavour of the TRC was bluntly rejected by some white people, including the former president P. W. Botha who called it a witch-hunt and a circus. For people like Botha, who defended apartheid by calling it 'good neighbourliness', the TRC brought neither the truth nor reconciliation. For many whites, facing up to what had been done in their name was a painful experience and many preferred not to know. Some groups, like the Dutch Reformed Church, who had defended apartheid, eventually came to admit that they had been wrong.

Reconciliation will be a long process for a country divided against itself, but the truth that came to light because of the TRC may prove to be an essential part of such a process. The abuses of justice committed under apartheid have been put on record and they stand as testimony for future generations. Although the TRC has been criticized for the way it worked, the atrocities it dealt with cannot be denied. The role of the government and its security forces in directing these atrocities has been established.

What remained disappointing was the inability of the National Party to accept responsibility for the injustices committed while it was in government. The tortures and murders were blamed on extremist individuals, not politicians. Even though those who tortured and killed thought they were carrying out what the government wanted, de Klerk would not accept responsibility. Tutu said, sarcastically, even before the hearings began: 'It is very difficult now to find anyone in South Africa

### Accepting responsibility

A woman in the public gallery during a TRC hearing expressed astonishment that so few white people accepted responsibility for what happened under apartheid:

'There are plenty of dead and damaged people ... but no guilty people. No one supported apartheid. It's denial on a grand scale. Pretty soon we will be talking about alleged apartheid.'
(Quoted in *The Independent*, 12 October 1996)

## 'Still feeling the pain'

Lizzie Sefola's husband, Harold, was taken away by the police and tortured before being killed. Appearing at the TRC, Lizzie said:

'We're still feeling the pain. These people never came to ask us for forgiveness. The government is doing this on our behalf ... It is people who should forgive each other, not the government.' (Quoted in Arnold, *The New South Africa*)

October 1998: documents are packed away as the TRC's work is finished.

who ever supported apartheid. Oh no, I never supported apartheid, I always knew it was wrong.' The TRC found it difficult to bring into the open all of those involved in atrocities, partly because tons of classified records and documents had already been destroyed by politicians and civil servants. These records included the names of the large number of black people who had informed on the ANC and acted as spies for the security forces.

## Becoming human again

Cynthia Ngewu, the mother of Christopher Piet who was shot by the police in March 1986, made this statement to the TRC:

'This thing called reconciliation ... if I am understanding it correctly ... if it means this man who has killed Christopher Piet, if it means he becomes human again, this man, so that I, so that all of us, get our humanity back ... then I agree, then I support it all.' (Quoted in Krog, *Country of My Skull*)

# RIGHTING THE WRONGS

## An ANC government

The burden of responsibility for righting the wrongs of apartheid lay with the ANC after their success in the 1994 election. For the first two years, the ANC had power as part of the Government of National Unity and, to begin with, there was a spirit of co-operation and reconciliation. ANC leaders, who had been labelled terrorists by white governments of the past, went out of their way to create an atmosphere of togetherness. When South Africa won the Rugby World Cup in 1995, Nelson Mandela appeared in the stadium wearing the rugby jersey of the winning Springbok team and he won acclaim from the largely white, Afrikaner crowd. The idea of a peaceful, multicultural society – a 'rainbow nation', as the idea was popularly called – began to seem a real possibility.

However, not everyone in the National Party could come to terms with an ANC government and in May 1996 the National Party withdrew from the Government of National Unity. This left the ANC running the government, along with the Inkatha party. The ANC was not like a political party in Western Europe or North America. Between 1960 and 1990 it had been a banned organization, and its leading members had no previous experience of running a country. The ANC had been a broad-based organization bringing together people who

June 1995: President Mandela hands the cup to the captain of the winning Springbok team, François Pienaar.

## 'Some people change'

An ANC activist who fought for the overthrow of apartheid explains how some of his colleagues changed when the fighting was over:

'It is interesting to see who still carries their own briefcase. These are people I've known for years when we were in the field. Some of them are still great but some of them have become very pompous. When you have a car and a driver and you're travelling first class, some people change.'
(Quoted in *The Guardian*, 16 May 2001)

opposed the apartheid state, and this created its sense of unity and purpose. Now it faced the task of governing and transforming a large and complex economy, and differences of opinion emerged about the best way forward.

### Making changes

The kind of changes that the ANC were planning were announced after the 1994 election in the form of a Reconstruction and Development Programme (RDP). The RDP set out principles for political and social reforms to create a more equal society. The first priority was said to be to meet basic needs – like water, electricity, health care and housing – for the majority of people who had suffered under apartheid. However, these good intentions were very slow to be translated into action and soon differences of opinion within the ANC became clear. One point of view was that South Africa's existing wealth should be redistributed in favour of the poor and dispossessed. This was seen as too socialist by others, who wanted to stimulate the economy in the hope of creating better conditions for reforms. By the middle of 1996, the RDP was more or less abandoned and a new programme was announced.

One *law* for one *nation*

At first, after the multiracial elections, there was great expectation that the wrongs of the past would be put right. This hope was expressed by crowds watching the signing of the new constitution in Sharpeville, 1996.

GEAR, standing for Growth, Employment and Redistribution, was the new government policy. It aimed to stimulate economic growth and thereby create thousands of new jobs. GEAR represented a rejection of the more radical, socialist measures that the ANC had once stood for. The policy looked to privatization and the free market as a means of encouraging economic growth. It was criticized by trade unions and other groups who felt the ANC were too willing to follow the advice of international capitalist organizations like the World Bank.

GEAR did not prove as successful as the government had been led to expect. The target economic growth rate of 6 per cent proved unachievable and, far from new jobs being created, unemployment remained a problem. One reason for the lack of new jobs was that foreign investment had not reached the levels that the government had planned. By 1998, the government had become alarmed at the rate of unemployment and promised to spend large amounts of money in order to create jobs. The criticism remained, however, that South Africa's economic problems could not be solved by relying on private investment and that the government should take a more active role to influence the economy.

Waiting for work outside a factory in Johannesburg, 1998.

Sewing clothes – a small business started with government support, Johannesburg, 1999.

## Affirmative action – at work

A lot of new legislation known as affirmative action was introduced to remove past inequalities. In 1998 a new law forced any company employing more than 50 people to show that it no longer discriminated against black people and women. Companies were given 18 months to show that they were making changes, but the pace of change has been very slow. Many companies dragged their feet in doing anything to change their employment practices and white people continued to benefit in terms of having a good job and being promoted within the company for which they worked. In many cases, white-owned companies made changes that made it seem as if they were complying with the law but in reality nothing was very different.

The government passed a law that created a special training fund for black workers, who in the past had been denied chances to improve their work skills and so gain promotion. In 2000 another law outlawed racial hate speech.

## The land

The government responded to the demands of black people who had claims on land taken from them in the past. It tried to restore the stolen land with the minimum amount of confrontation with white farmers, by offering compensation and carefully observing legal procedures.

### Payback time

Deon Welz lives and works in Cape Town in the legal profession. Unlike many whites, he accepts the need for affirmative action in order to deal with the legacy of apartheid:

'We [white people] benefited from the apartheid regime and now it's payback time.'
(Quoted in *The Independent*, 5 August 2000)

Once a labourer on someone else's land, this man in Kwa-Zulu Natal in 1998 is now a sugar farmer in his own right.

Wherever possible, the aim was to create a 'willing seller, willing buyer' atmosphere. It was 2001 before the first case arose where land taken from blacks under apartheid was forcibly returned to its owners. This case involved a large farm, about 150 miles northeast of Johannesburg. It belonged to a black community of 600 families who had been forced to leave the land in 1957.

By 1999, over 70,000 families had been settled on about 1.5 per cent of agricultural land – a long way from the goal of the RDP to redistribute about 30 per cent of agricultural land within five years of the election. It will take a long time before that figure is reached, but there are well over 20,000 cases still being processed.

## Who owns the land?

A black South African asserted his right to land of which white farmers have legal ownership:

'The very same documents that are in their [white people's] possession were issued to them without consulting the owners of the land ... They did not buy the land from us and therefore they cannot tell us about title deeds. Our forefathers are buried there.'

Another claimant feels equally certain about his right to the land: 'There is absolutely no point in discussing the issue of title deeds because we were forcibly removed. Those who dispossessed us of our land should be the ones subjected to questions.'
(Quoted in Levin and Weiner, *No More Tears*)

# '/aise'

/Guna Rooi, aged 70, hugged the then deputy president Thabo Mbeki on behalf of the San people receiving their land back and said (the slash represents a click in her language):

'/aise' [thank you]

Her friend, Anna Kassie, summed up her feelings about her land and language:

'When I am no longer here, and I die, I want it to be known in my language that this was our land.'
(Quoted in *The Independent*, 22 March 1999)

In 1995, some white farmers decided to leave the new South Africa and trek north to establish new farms elsewhere. They were consciously imitating the Great Trek of the nineteenth century. Four neighbouring African countries let them settle, in the hope that their farming experience would benefit them.

In 1999, a more significant event took place when relatively large areas of land were returned to communities who had had it taken from them in the past by Afrikaner governments. The Khomani clan, who belonged to the nearly-extinct San people of southern Africa, had 155,000 acres of land returned to them. These San people live in the southern Kalahari, a large desert region of southern Africa. An equal amount of land was given to the 5,000-strong Mier community who, like the Khomani, had been expelled from their land between 1931 and 1973.

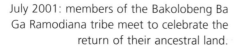

July 2001: members of the Bakolobeng Ba Ga Ramodiana tribe meet to celebrate the return of their ancestral land.

Learning cricket and togetherness at a school near Johannesburg, 1996.

## Affirmative action in sport

Affirmative action has been taken to deal with the fact that black players are under-represented in the country's rugby and cricket teams. In order to achieve a situation where black players are part of South Africa's national teams, regulations have been made that all school rugby teams must include a certain number of non-white players. Another regulation is that all provincial cricket teams must now have at least one non-white player. South Africa's national rugby and cricket teams remain predominantly white, but over time this will change.

Breyton Paulse during the first match of the Rugby World Cup Sevens, 2001.

### Old attitudes

Luyuyo Matsha works for an organization seeking to increase the number of black players playing rugby in South Africa. Here he expresses his frustration at the slow pace of change:

'There are people in rugby who are holding on to the old days, who want to block development. They feel that blacks are now trying to rob them of the last thing they have.'
(Quoted in *The Guardian*, 26 February 1999)

## Catching up

South Africa is a rich country in terms of its natural resources and work force but very poor in terms of basic services for all its citizens. New York's Manhattan Island, for example, has more telephones than in the whole of Africa south of the Sahara desert. By 1999, the South African government was able to claim that in the five years since the election an average of 750 telephones per day had been installed. Over the same period, an average of 1,300 homes per day were connected to an electricity supply and 1,700 people per day provided with access to clean water. New clinics treated 8.5 million patients in the first four years after 1994 and in 1995 a polio-hepatitis vaccination programme began, immunizing 8 million children in two years.

April 1999: a tap provided by the government saves walking one kilometre to the nearest waterpoint.

## Beautiful toilets

Jeanette Ngora works as a cleaner and child minder and lives in an inner-city district of Johannesburg where the crime rate is very high.

'My parents live in a village near King Williamstown and I used to be scared to visit when it was dark because the only light came from candles and fires. Last year, they got electricity and running water for the first time and a clinic will be built in their area, and it's made a huge difference to their lives. This year they're getting toilets, which will be beautiful.'
(Quoted in *Gemini News Service*, 11 April 1998)

The shortage of adequate housing was also addressed and by 1999 some 3 million people had been rehoused. More classrooms were built, and about 1.5 million new pupils had gained access to the education system by 1999. The government's aim to provide ten years of compulsory free education for every South African child has almost been achieved. On the other hand, it has proved difficult to break down the way that apartheid created good schools in white neighbourhoods and poor ones in black areas.

Top: bricklayers at work on a low-cost housing project in Alexandra township, 1999.

Above: inside a new government home.

Right: The first computers at a township school in Cape Town – part of a project funded by the Dutch government.

Rough diamonds from the area near Cape Town. The largest weighs 32 carats.

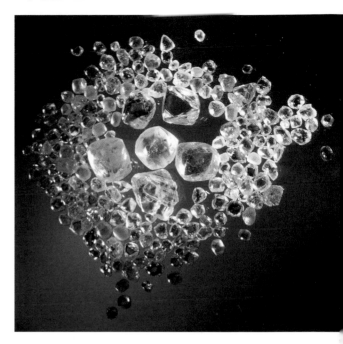

## Sharing the diamonds

South Africa has some of the world's richest mineral reserves, including diamonds, gold, platinum, uranium and manganese. In most countries, mineral rights belong to the state and private companies make deals with the government to obtain mining licences. In South Africa it is different because private companies own the mineral rights for themselves. This deprives the state of revenue and, because most of the mines are owned by whites, makes it very difficult for black business people to find a way into the market. The ANC has introduced legislation, known unofficially as the 'Robin Hood' law, which will abolish the private ownership of mineral rights and give them to the state, which will then award licences to companies.

The ANC legislation, planned to become law in 2002, will allow the state to grant mining licences lasting 25 years. In the interests of racial equality, companies seeking a licence will have to show that they are promoting black participation in their organizations. Black companies will have an advantage in applying for licences and the government will have the right to take over mines that fail to meet their obligations. The small number of white-owned mining companies, who own most of the country's mineral rights, oppose the legislation and are trying to weaken it by arguing that it is unfair.

## Mining rights

Tokyo Sexwale is a black businessman whose company is hoping to gain a stake in his country's diamond and platinum industry. This is what he said about De Beers and Anglo Gold, two powerful, white-owned mining companies that own a large percentage of South Africa's mineral rights:

'[They] are bent on frustrating black business ... [and] behave as if the country still belongs to them ... they use all sorts of stratagems to keep new entrants out.'
(Quoted in *The Times*, 7 February 2001)

# LOOKING TO THE FUTURE

## New elections

South Africa's second multiracial elections took place in 1999 and it was no surprise that the ANC emerged as the party with the most votes. Indeed, the ANC emerged as a stronger party of government than before because it now had a two-thirds majority in parliament, and this meant it could make changes to the constitution. The ANC also won control of KwaZulu Natal from the Inkatha Freedom Party (IFP). This strengthened the ANC considerably and brought to an end the bitter rivalry between itself and the Inkatha party, a rivalry that had claimed at least 10,000 lives over the past fifteen years.

### A change of attitude

Simphiwe Mhlati, living in one of the former 'homelands', approached the 1999 election with a different attitude from before:

'In 1994 we didn't vote for policies, or even a vision. We voted for a man. There is a lot of frustration now. I think in the next election we will be looking at policies. If somebody gives us a good promise, we will go for it.'
(Quoted in Bell, *Somewhere Over the Rainbow*)

Nelson Mandela and Thabo Mbeki at an election rally in Soweto, March 1999.

The 1999 elections also served as the occasion for the retirement of Nelson Mandela as president of South Africa. Mandela had come to be regarded like a saint for the way he had steered his country towards peaceful change. He summed up his country's achievement: 'For a country that was the polecat of the world ... the doors of the world have opened, precisely because of our success in achieving things that humanity as a whole holds dear.'

Thabo Mbeki, his former deputy president, became the new president of South Africa. Mbcki had not spent 27 years in prison like Mandela, but he had also paid a very high price for his opposition to the white government. Both his son and his brother died in the fight against apartheid and Mbeki himself spent 30 years in exile. He said: 'The dismal shame of poverty, suffering and human degradation of my continent is a blight that we share ... This is a savage road to which nobody should be condemned.'

The commanding position held by the ANC has led critics to claim that the country's democracy is in danger because one party dominates parliament. They point to events in nearby

## Voting in 1999

Maria Zulu, voting in 1999 for the second time in her life, felt optimistic about the future:

'Before, things could be very difficult. I am a Zulu but used to have lots of friends and family who were Xhosas. For a while, I didn't want to see them because I was afraid something would happen to them or me. But things are calmer now. You don't have to be suspicious any more.'

Maria wouldn't say who she was voting for but when she compared Nelson Mandela with Moses there was little doubt that the ANC would receive her vote:

'He [Mandela] has come and delivered his children. I think he is the chosen one who is taking us – maybe not to a promised land – but to a better place.'
(Quoted in *The Guardian*, 28 May 1999)

Tony Leon (right), leader of the Democratic Party, dances with party workers in a mixed-race area near Johannesburg, 1999.

Zimbabwe and suggest that something similar could happen in South Africa. In Zimbabwe, the party that overthrew the rule of a white minority is accused of turning itself into a dictatorship by using its strong position to crush any opposition. Although possible, this seems unlikely to happen in South Africa in the foreseeable future. The country has a strong democratic constitution, there are well-organized trade unions and there is a new opposition party, the Democratic Alliance, that makes itself heard.

The National Party went through a period of inner conflict in the years after the 1994 election. It was divided between a right wing, who never really gave up thinking that apartheid was a good system, and a more moderate wing willing to come to terms with the new South Africa. Eventually, in 2000, the National Party merged with another small party of the white minority, the Democratic Party, and formed the Democratic Alliance. This new party set out to appeal to Asians and those of mixed descent, as well as to its traditional white supporters, and in local council elections at the end of 2000 it won more than a quarter of the votes. However, it will not be able to capture national power without a big increase in support from black people, and this seems unlikely for the foreseeable future. The council elections in 2000 did suggest that a number of black voters chose to stay at home and not bother voting for the ANC.

## Challenges ahead

The results of a survey of 30,000 households were published in 2000 and showed that black South Africans still have a long way to go to catch up with the standard of living enjoyed by most whites in the country. The average white pay packet is ten times the average black wage and eight million blacks live on less than a dollar a day. Only 17 per cent of black families have flush lavatories and fewer than three in five live in properly built houses. Unemployment amongst blacks runs at nearly 30 per cent and a black person is six times more likely than a white person to be without a job. Of the estimated 2.4 million households living below the poverty line, only 2 per cent are white. There are still village schools with classes of 50 and with no textbooks, no library, no toilet and insufficient desks.

South Africa is still faced with the challenge of removing the legacy of apartheid and colonialism. The white minority, some four million people in a land of over 40 million, continues jealously to guard its wealth. Under apartheid, white people were brought up to think that black people were inferior, and it will take another generation at least before the psychological scars of apartheid are removed.

Every now and again, incidents occur that remind everyone that racism is still a cruel factor in South African life. In a tragic case in 1998 a black baby named Angelina was shot dead by the white farmer who employed her family. In court, the farmer claimed that he had fired into the air to warn off what he thought were intruders, but a witness

## 'Things will improve'

One of a group of black youngsters in the village where baby Angelina was killed expressed their feelings about the future:

'Things will improve. At least now we have the same rights as whites and quite a lot of them do not expect us to call them 'baas' [Afrikaans for 'master']. People are not changing as fast as the law, but they will.'
(Quoted in *The Times* 15 June 1999)

At the funeral of six-month-old Angelina Zwane, April 1998.

suggested he had been drinking and knew there were no intruders. The Afrikaner judge called it an accident and gave the farmer a suspended prison sentence. 'If he'd been a black man who had killed a white baby, they would have put him away for 90 years,' said an angry resident in the neighbourhood. The controversial case led to demands that some of the white judges, who were appointed for life, should be forced to retire. People remembered that judges refused to appear at the Truth and Reconciliation Commission.

In another case in 2001, nine white players from a rugby club were put on trial for beating to death a black youth. At first they expected to be released on bail and appeared in court laughing. However, one confessed to the crime and angry crowds gathered outside insisting that bail should not be offered.

A case like this reflects the fact that the legacy of apartheid still divides part of South Africa. One survey showed that while 76 per cent of blacks approved of the work of the Truth and Reconciliation Commission, only 37 per cent of whites did. In a 2001 survey of nearly 4,000 people, just over half of the blacks found it hard to imagine being friends with a white and over half thought whites were untrustworthy. Equal proportions of whites and blacks – just under 20 per cent – thought the country would be better off without the other group.

## A racist crime

When nine rugby players appeared in court in April 2001 over the death of a young black man, angry crowds gathered outside the courtroom. Thomas Ramaloko, expressed what most of them were thinking:

'These Boers commit a heinous crime knowing their brothers will let them off. The Boers still think they have the power. He died a terrible death. There's no doubt this was racially motivated.' (Quoted in *The Guardian*, 7 April 2001)

Friends sharing soccer fever.

Lawlessness and crime continue to be a major problem and the failure to reduce unemployment only makes it worse. South Africa's total of 25,000 murders a year is over six times higher than in the USA, a country that is some seven times larger. The World Health Organization says that South Africa is the world's most violent society not at war. A rape is committed every 30 seconds in South Africa. There are three times as many security guards as there are police, and vigilante groups operate in some neighbourhoods. One large vigilante organization in the north of the country, claiming 35,000 members, administers beatings on a regular basis to suspected criminals. The favourite weapon used during these beatings is the sjambok, a stiff leather South African whip.

## Living with crime

The home of the Morrell family has a private guard who signs visitors in and out, but Mr Morrell was still robbed at gunpoint in his garage. His wife has adjusted to the risk of crime:

'To get my car insurance, I had to go on an anti-hijacking course. But that's the way things are now.'
(Quoted in *The Guardian*, 28 May 1999)

With his brother, John Gibb set up a group of vigilantes in Durban, in 1995. They patrol the beachfront with batons and whips.

## Rough justice

Boet Erasmus is a white South African vigilante who has taken part in beatings of suspected criminals:

'With the first hiding you soon find out if you've got the wrong guy. It takes about 10 minutes. Then we give it a break and give him another 10 minutes. They yelp something terrible. If they're guilty they soon tell you where the goods are.'
(Quoted in *The Guardian*, 12 May 1999)

At the AIDS conference in Durban in 2000, Nkosi Johnson said of people with HIV and AIDS: 'Care for us and accept us – we are all human beings, we are normal, we have hands, we have feet, we can walk, we can talk, we have needs just like everyone else. Don't be afraid of us – we are all the same.'

Vigilante groups are accused of torture and killing, but businesses pay them large sums of money every month for protection. In Cape Town an organization called PAGAD – People Against Gangsters and Drugs – is thought to be responsible for the killing of scores of gang leaders in the area.

## A million orphans

There is an AIDS epidemic throughout Africa, where two-thirds of all hospital beds are occupied by people with AIDS-related illness, but South Africa was late in recognizing the problem. Infection with HIV, the virus that causes AIDS, is growing at a faster rate in South Africa than anywhere else in the world. It is predicted that within a few years AIDS will reduce the average life expectancy for black people in South Africa from 60 years to 40. Across Africa, an estimated six million children have lost one or both of their parents to AIDS. South Africa faces the prospect of having one million AIDS orphans. Drugs that combat AIDS are too expensive to give out to the more-than four million South Africans who are HIV-positive, and only about 10,000 of them can afford to buy the drugs.

The international pharmaceutical companies that produce drugs for treating AIDS took South Africa to court in 2001 for importing cheap versions of the drugs from other countries. The companies claimed that South Africa should not be allowed to do this and should pay the same high prices for the drugs as Western countries. After much bad publicity for their attitude, they dropped the court case and South Africa was able to import and manufacture the cheaper drugs.

Remarkably, it took a 12-year-old boy, dying of the disease, to bring home to South Africa the seriousness of the AIDS epidemic. Nkosi Johnson made a dramatic appearance at the world's biggest AIDS conference in Durban in 2000 and called on President Mbeki to do more to combat the disease. Nkosi first came to public attention in 1997 when parents protested at his presence in school because of his HIV status. By the time Nkosi died, in June 2001, his country was much more aware of the urgent need to combat AIDS.

## South Africa today

The 2000 survey of households also asked people how they felt about the quality of their lives and whether they were optimistic about the future. Whites and Asians saw themselves as 'losers' in the new South Africa and were pessimistic about the future. The survey described such groups, enjoying a good standard of living but fearful of losing it, as the 'whining well'. The attitude of many whites was summed up by one person's comment: 'Most whites in this country want to emigrate. But not to America, or Britain, or New Zealand or Australia. They want to emigrate to the old South Africa.'

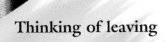

## Thinking of leaving

Margie Morrell, a physiotherapist living in a wealthy white suburb with both a gardener and a maid, thought about leaving:

'A lot of people keep saying to us, "You must leave, you must leave", and we have been thinking about it ... But at the moment, the lifestyle here is better than anywhere else in the world.'
(Quoted in *The Guardian*, 28 May 1999)

Whites living in a poor area, 2001.

## Poor whites

Before 1994, even the least educated or least able whites could benefit from apartheid. Afterwards, with jobs no longer guaranteed, some – like 33-year-old Sonia Scnekal – found it difficult to adjust:

'Sometimes I just cry because I cannot take all this ... If I could go tomorrow I would. We were saving up to leave South Africa but we used up every penny when my husband became unemployed.'
(Quoted in *The Independent*, 12 February 1998)

## Fears

Mr Kallideen, an Indian South African, expressed his concern for the future of his country:

'There is a fear of affirmative action, this business of allocating jobs on the basis of race rather than skills. Once you begin to put the wrong people in places of authority, confidence goes down. Although the economy is still strong, it must be looked after by the right people. What we are fearing is that it must not go the Africa way, you know. If there is fraud and stealing from government coffers, the whole country will be dragged down. Then the young people will leave.'
(Quoted in Bell, *Somewhere Over the Rainbow*)

People classified as coloureds in South Africa, those of mixed descent, have often felt left out and isolated in their country. Under apartheid, they also faced discrimination, but many did not ally themselves with the ANC and in the 1994 election the majority voted for the National Party. Most coloureds now vote for the Democratic Alliance.

Of those in the survey who expressed optimism about the future, one in three were the very poor. People who have the least look

## Waiting

Ann Jaar, aged 63, lives with her three adult children and two grandchildren in a bamboo house with an outside tap. Her fourth daughter was murdered in 1999 and a third grandchild is in prison for burglary. She remained optimistic:

'I can't work any more. My arms are giving in, and my legs. I have grown too old to wash people's clothes. I do feel that things will come right. We will just have to wait and see.'
(Quoted in *The Independent*, 5 August 2000)

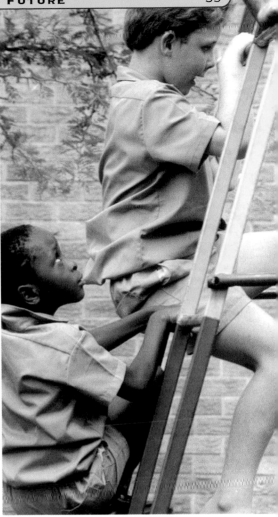

White people in South Africa remain at the top of the economic ladder, but the rest of the population are waiting for their just share of the country's prosperity.

forward to small gains, like electricity and free schooling, and remain hopeful that the future will bring an improvement. Gaining the vote in 1994 brought a sense of dignity to millions of black people, but they are now looking to build upon this sense of dignity. Nelson Mandela recognized this in his last speech as party leader when he attacked white parties and the white-owned media for always running down their country. Many supporters of the ANC feel that the new South Africa has gone out of its way to accommodate the white minority and that the time has now come to go beyond just talk about a rainbow nation.

The euphoria and excitement that followed the 1994 election have passed into history. South Africa can feel justly proud of having peacefully created a multiracial nation, avoiding the bloodbath that its grim history seemed to predict. This was an extraordinary event. Its people now look forward to a more equal society. They want what is due.

### Truth and reality

William Makgoba, a professor at a South African university, gave his opinion of the new South Africa:

'The truth and reality in South Africa today and into the future is no longer European or white, but African and more often black. The sooner the opposition parties get this message, the better. The days of white politics, white privilege, white constituency and white truth are over and will never return.'
(Quoted in Spence, ed., *After Mandela*)

# DATE LIST

**1652**    Dutch colonists establish a settlement in what is now South Africa.

**1795**    The British arrive and by 1814 take over part of what is now South Africa.

**1836**    The start of the Great Trek by Afrikaner Boers.

**1886**    Diamonds are discovered and, two years later, gold also.

**1880-1 and 1899-1902**    Two Boer Wars between the British and Afrikaners.

**1910**    The Union of South Africa, a dominion of the British Empire, is formed and power is concentrated in an all-white parliament.

**1913**    Natives Land Act, and another one in 1936, allocates just 13 per cent of land to black use.

**1937**    A system of pass laws is extended throughout South Africa.

**1948**    The National Party gains power and extends racist legislation into a system of apartheid.

**1949**    Inter-racial marriages are banned.

**1953**    Racial segregation in schools is enforced.

**1960**    At Sharpeville, police kill 68 people protesting against pass laws.

**1961**    South Africa leaves the Commonwealth and becomes an independent republic.

**1962**    Nelson Mandela is arrested and imprisoned.

**1970**    Every black is made a citizen of one of the 'homelands'.

**1976**    Many killed in Soweto resisting the teaching of Afrikaans in schools.

**1980s**    Uprisings and civil unrest in black neighbourhoods against the apartheid state. International protests and sanctions against South Africa.

**1989**    A new president, F. W. de Klerk, promises a new South Africa.

**1990**    Mandela is released from prison and negotiations begin between the ANC and the white government.

**1994**    First multiracial general election, with the ANC winning a large majority. Government of National Unity formed.

**1996-8** The Truth and Reconciliation Commission collects testimonies from the apartheid era.

**1999** Second multiracial general election, with the ANC again winning a large majority.

**2000** Nkosi Johnson, dying of AIDS at 12 years of age, calls on the government to do more to help AIDS victims.

**2001** International pharmaceutical companies drop court action to prevent the government importing cheap drugs to deal with AIDS.

# RESOURCES

**Further Reading**

*Changing Face of South Africa* by Rob Bowden and Tony Binns (Hodder Wayland, 2001)

*Country of My Skull* by Antjie Krog (Vintage, 1999) tells the story of the Truth and Reconciliation Commission. Many testimonies, painful to read, from the oppressed and oppressors.

*Country Studies: South Africa* by Garrett Nagle (Heinemann Library, 1999) describes the physical, human and environmental geography of South Africa.

*Famous Lives: Nelson Mandela* (Hodder Wayland, 2000) tells the story of the man who spent 10,000 days in prison before being freed to become president of his country

*Miriam's Song* by Miriam Mathabane (Simon & Schuster, 2000), as told to Mark Mathabane, is the memoir of a young black woman growing up in South Africa in the 1980s. It creates a sense of the civil unrest that was tearing the country apart as black people struggled against the apartheid regime.

*Rainbow Nation Revisited* by Donald Woods (André Deutsch, 2000) recounts a return visit to South Africa by a journalist who fled the country in 1970. He compares the present with the past and considers what the future holds.

*The New South Africa* by Guy Arnold (Macmillan, 2000) looks at different aspects of South Africa's economy and society during the period of Mandela's presidency. Lots of facts and figures, looking at the challenges facing Mbeki's government.

*Survivors: A Long Walk to Lavender Street: A Story from South Africa* by Belinda Hollyer (Hodder Wayland, 2002)

**Film**

*Long Night's Journey into Day*, directed by Frances Reid and Deborah Hoffmann, USA, 2000. This documentary looks at some cases from the Truth and Reconciliation Commission, including a South African policeman seeking amnesty for killing an activist and the parents of a Fulbright scholar murdered in South Africa, who return to the country to confront the killers.

**Websites**

http://www.irisfilms.org/longnight/index.htm
A website for the *Long Night's Journey into Day* documentary film.

http://www.truth.org.za/
A site dedicated to the Truth and Reconciliation Commission, with transcripts and links to other sites about South Africa.

http://www.southafrica.co.za/
A general information site about South Africa with news, reference, government, education, leisure and lifestyle.

http://www.anc.org.za/
The official ANC site with links to related internet resources, including a picture library.

For a list of sources from which quotations have been included in this book, see page 64.

# GLOSSARY

**activist** someone taking vigorous action on behalf of something they believe in.

**affirmative action** special legislation to remove social and economic inequalities.

**Afrikaners** descendants of Europeans who had been born in the Dutch colony in southern Africa, and were therefore 'Africans'; also known as Boers (the Dutch word for 'farmers').

**AIDS** acquired immune deficiency syndrome – a fatal disease caused by HIV, the human immunodeficiency virus, transmitted in the blood.

**ANC** African National Congress, the governing party of South Africa; founded in 1912 as a liberation movement and banned between 1960 and 1990.

**apartheid** system of racial discrimination practised in South Africa under the National Party, which ruled between 1948 and 1994.

**Boers** *see* Afrikaners.

**capital** money, wealth for investment.

**coloureds** an official term used by the apartheid South African state to label citizens of mixed descent.

**homelands** specially designated areas of countryside where black people were forced to live in apartheid South Africa.

**Inkatha Freedeom Party** the political party of the Zulu people, under the leadership of Mangosuthu Buthelezi. Inkatha is the Zulus' word for 'peace'.

**National Party** the former governing party, responsible for implementing apartheid in South Africa.

**neo-Nazi** having extreme racist views, often accompanied by brutal behaviour.

**pass laws** a system of laws, introduced in the 1930s, that restricted the right of black people to travel in South Africa. Special passes allowed non-white people to travel outside homelands and townships for the purpose of employment.

**privatization** the process of taking something into the ownership of a private company, as opposed to its being owned by the state.

**racism** a belief in the superiority of a particular race.

**Rand** the currency of South Africa.

**segregation** forcing racial groups to live separately in a community.

**shanty town** a poor and depressed area with inadequate housing.

**socialism** the belief that society should be organized around common or state ownership and not on the basis of private ownership.

**townships** specially designated urban areas where black people were forced to live in apartheid South Africa.

**Xhosa** the name of the majority of people in South Africa, speaking the Xhosa language, as opposed to the minority Zulu people.

**Zulus** an African people who formed a kingdom in the nineteenth century. Their territory was much reduced in size after their defeat by the Boers and the British and became one of the 'homelands' of South Africa, known as KwaZulu.

# INDEX

# SOURCES

Sources of information for this book were:
Guy Arnold, *The New South Africa*, Macmillan, 2000
Gavin Bell, *Somewhere Over the Rainbow*, Abacus, 2000
Richard Buckley, ed., *South Africa After Apartheid, Understanding Global Issues*, European Schoolbooks Publishing, 1995
Rodney Davenport and Christopher Saunders, *South Africa*, Macmillan 2000
Fergal Keane, *The Bondage of Fear*, Viking, 1994
Antjie Krog, *Country of My Skull*, Vintage, 1999
Alan Lester, Etienne Nel and Tony Binns, *South Africa Past, Present and Future*, Pearson Education, 2000
Richard Levin and Daniel Weiner, ed., *'No More Tears ...': Struggles for Land in Mpumalanga, South Africa*, Africa World Press, 1997
Miriam Mathabane, *Miriam's Song*, Simon & Schuster, 2000
Julian May, ed., *Poverty and Inequality in South Africa: Meeting the Challenge*, Zed Books, 2000
Martin J. Murray, *The Revolution Deferred*, Verso, 1994
J. E. Spence, ed., *After Mandela*, Royal Institute of International Affairs, 1999
Charles Villa-Vicencio and Wilhelm Verwoerd, *Looking Back Reaching Forward*, Zed Books, 2000
Donald Woods, *Rainbow Nation Revisited*, André Deutsch, 2000